The Little Book of
LEFTOVERS

Kevin Crafts

Crown Trade Paperbacks
New York

Published by Crown Trade Paperbacks, 201 East 50th Street, New York, New York 10022.
Member of the Crown Publishing Group.
Random House, Inc. New York, Toronto, London, Sydney, Auckland

CROWN TRADE PAPERBACKS and colophon are trademarks of Crown Publishers, Inc.
Manufactured in the United States of America

Design by Lisa Goldenberg

Library of Congress Cataloging-in-Publication Data
Crafts, Kevin
The little book of leftovers/Kevin Crafts.
Includes index.
1. Cookery (Leftovers) I. Title.
TX652.C773 1994   94–7896
641. 5'52—dc20   CIP

ISBN 0-517-88198-5
10 9 8 7 6 5 4 3 2 1
First Edition

This book is dedicated
to my parents,
Cliff and Eileen,
for teaching me how to love
— without question —
a house full of people

contents

A VIEW FROM THE fridge

I used to wait each year for Academy Awards night to defrost my freezer. Both the awards presentation and the process of defrosting seemed pretty endless, generated the same meager amount of enjoyment, demanded the same half-hearted attention, and usually lasted until after midnight.

Throughout the year, my fridge became a dump site for all the foods I stored as "leftovers" or bought in abundance during some short-lived spasm of gastronomic aspiration.

As the evening progressed and the ice gradually melted, the previous year was relived before my eyes in the form of strangely colored and slightly furry meats and vegetables. By the time the Best Picture Oscar had been awarded I would be knee-deep in a puddle of defrosting memories that more closely resembled fossils of the Precambrian Era than Leftover Hamburger Patties, Flounder Provençale, or Lentil Soup (I was never able to confirm that one for sure).

I remember throwing away a badly freezer-burned roast as Sally Field uttered those now-famous words, "You like me, you really like me!" It was then I realized that there might be some "leftover" management skills I had been missing out on. As I started to unwrap one of the many other foil-clad artifacts, I wondered not only how old its contents were in dog years, but also why my refrigerator continually became a morgue for things like old wedding cake or ham bones collected in hopes of making stock or bean soup. Perhaps what was needed was some sort of Twelve-step Program of food storage and preservation.

I came to the conclusion that there had to be a relatively painless way to create easily prepared meals for multiple occasions and use surplus foods creatively instead of threatening the environment every time I cleaned out the icebox. By properly preparing and storing selected foods, I would not only be able to curb those nightly trips to the market but I'd be able to stockpile many of my favorite items for actual consumption—and all that I needed to do was to create and adhere to a few basic guidelines. I knew that this would never be a cuisine destined for air-kissing friends to be served with memorable wines or fine china, but just because these foods carried the slightly unromantic label of "leftovers" was no reason why they couldn't be just as spectacular the second time around.

As a habitual grocery shopper, I carefully started shopping for both the present and the future and rationally thought about "economical" bulk purchases. I learned to avoid buying mass quantities of foods with short shelf lives (dairy products come to mind). Yes, it may seem thrifty to buy a quart of ricotta cheese, but if you use only a total of 2 cups over the course of two weeks, you end up throwing half away. Where's the savings?

I thought twice before casually tossing away foods that were a few days shy of going bad or were significantly bruised; bruises on fruits and vegetables can be pared away and the rest can be used to make gravies, sorbets, and stocks.

I took a few tips from the environmental and recycling enthusiasts and also learned about correct storage procedures and the shelf life of products. Why use foil or plastic wraps only once when a small collection of resealable plastic containers actually keep foods better, and as a bonus, can be passed on to grandchildren like heirloom china.

As I no longer need to spend that wintry Monday evening every March waiting for both the ice to melt and the Best Sound Editing in a Foreign Film award, I am amazed at how changing a few old habits and reviewing the contents of both the refrigerator and freezer every few weeks, my culinary existence has taken on an exciting and even economical new twist. So, with renewed fervor, I offer some practical and evocative uses for leftovers.

pantry

A few things you *might* want to have around

BROTH, whether homemade (see page 19) or canned, comes in handy for poaching poultry and fish, adding moisture without fat to sautéed dishes, and, of course, as the base for soups of all kinds. Keep a couple of cans of vegetable, chicken, and/or beef broth in your cupboard and you won't be sorry.

BUTTER lasts for weeks if stored correctly in a butter dish, or tightly wrapped, or for almost a lifetime in the freezer.

CANNED BEANS are high in fiber, affordable, and have a million uses. They should be well rinsed in cold water before use, as they are most often stored in a lovely viscous liquid that sometimes contains MSG. Canned beans may be added to salads, soups, and Mexican concoctions at will.

CANNED MUSHROOMS are not as good as fresh ones but are still great to add to pasta dishes, meat loaf, or most casseroles. They are usually available in small cans or jars, minimizing waste and preventing further leftover cycles (we like that).

CANNED WHOLE MILK OR POWDERED DRY MILK are good to have on hand as decent substitutes for heavy creams or other dairy products that have a limited lifetime. They also obliterate the "lipstick on the milk carton" issue completely.

CANNED WHOLE TOMATOES are half the work and sometimes far more flavorful than out-of-season supermarket tomatoes that are beautifully red on the outside and white, mealy, and flavorless inside.

DIJON MUSTARD will revive even the sorriest sauce, making it an important component of every pantry. It might be considered the Ace bandage of the Culinary First Aid kit, and should be used with great generosity and frequency.

DRIED HERBS *The general rule of thumb here is to use 1 teaspoon of dried herbs for every 2½ teaspoons fresh.*

    Basil We know basil, in its fresh form, as the most active ingredient in pesto sauce. This cousin of the mint family possesses the same kind of bold and apparent flavor, and is most common to savory dishes, especially Italian and French.

    Bay Leaf is the culinary good luck charm used to flavor stews, stocks, and sauces. It is usually used whole in its dried form, so it is easily retrieved and discarded before serving.

Dill While fresh dill often loses most of its flavor when heated and is most often added at the end of preparation, dried dill, although just as delicate, will better stand up to heat. It is a great addition to salad dressings and mustards as well as egg dishes and is a great way to personalize jarred mayonnaise.

Oregano Common to pizza, lasagna, and many foods of Italian descent, oregano is also fantastic used in conjunction with parsley, basil, tarragon, rosemary, thyme, and many other leafy herbs.

Parsley is perhaps the most common of the dried herbs, as it is a terrific enhancer of most savory dishes. This all-purpose herb adds both subtle flavor and color.

Rosemary With its sturdy leaves and hardy scent, rosemary can be used in a variety of dishes from soups to stews to roasted or grilled meat, fish, vegetables, and poultry. It can even add a new dimension to some fruit desserts.

Sage Sage works almost as well in its dried (not powdered) form as it does fresh. It can be used in poultry dishes for both stuffings and gravies, as well as a seasoning for any savory meat, fish, or vegetable. Sage is surprisingly effective in a Bloody Mary, should you be at a momentary loss for a stalk of celery, a wedge of lime, or a grind of pepper.

Tarragon is widely used in classic French dishes. It has a delicate flavor and is a great addition to salad dressings, egg dishes, sauces, and can be used for infusing oils and vinegars as well. Buy either the dried whole leaves or crushed leaves.

Thyme Thyme's woodsy flavor and fragrance will gracefully enhance everything from omelets to meat, fish, and poultry and it makes a great seasoning for stocks and soups. Like rosemary and sage, when dried its flavor remains more intact than some more delicate herbs.

EGGS have a multitude of purposes and last up to 3 to 4 weeks in the fridge stored in their original carton. Eggs should be kept in the back of the refrigerator rather than in the egg cubicles in the door, where temperatures can fluctuate each time the refrigerator is opened.

FROZEN VEGETABLES Many frozen vegetables, such as peas, corn, and string beans, are often preferable to canned as they are packaged in their purest form. Also, it's easier to use and preserve a half a box of a frozen vegetable than a half a can.

FROZEN PUFF-PASTRY SHEETS, PHYLLO DOUGH, PIZZA DOUGH, PIE CRUSTS, AND WONTON SKINS Almost any relic can be wrapped and baked in one of these store-bought or prepared doughs. They can magically turn random kitchen scraps into an hors d'oeuvre, main course, or dessert for a delicious command performance.

GARLIC will not only ward off evil spirits, but its flavor easily enhances practically any savory dish. Use only the fresh cloves, not the jarred kind. Sliced garlic can be added to a bottle of your favorite extra-virgin olive oil, and the garlic-infused oil can be used in salad dressings and sauces. It can also be added to good wine vinegars to enliven a salad dressing.

HOT PEPPER SAUCE This can brighten up a plethora of foods, from eggs to fish to poultry to dressings to sauces to meats—and so on. I personally like Tabasco sauce, the king of pepper sauces, the best.

KOSHER SALT is coarser than table salt, lending texture to things like the crispy skins of chicken and fish, and adds an extra boost of flavor to meats of all kinds.

LEMONS (BOTH JUICE AND ZEST) The juice isn't just a great enhancer of both sweet and savory flavors; it also keeps fruit like sliced bananas or apples from browning quickly. Freshly squeezed juice is far better than the bottled version. The zest adds spark to everything from soups to salad dressings to fruit cobblers.

LONG AND SHORT DRY PASTA Pasta in any shape or form makes a delicious and versatile first or main course, and can stretch leftovers like nobody's business.

OIL Although oil is perhaps one of our most familiar cooking mediums besides butter, it should be used in moderation as it is high in both fat and calories. However, the purchase of good bottles of both vegetable oil and extra-virgin olive oil is highly recommended—in addition to whatever oil has caught your fancy at the moment, of course.

PARMESAN, ROMANO, OR ASIAGO CHEESE is best when purchased in large chunks, stored tightly wrapped in the freezer, then freshly grated just before serving. Leftover rinds or skins of many aged cheeses can be stored in the freezer and then crumbled on top of piping hot soups and stews before serving.

RICE Like pasta, rice serves a multitude of purposes and appetites and can turn leftovers into a complete main dish. Among the varieties you might want to keep on hand are long- or medium-grain white or brown rice, short-grain Italian Arborio rice, Indian or Pakistani basmati rice, and perhaps even wild rice—which is not a true rice but a grain.

SOY SAUCE, be it in leftover plastic packets from the nearest Chinese restaurant or purchased in a bottle, is a great seasoning and allows you to cut back on fatty oils or butter. You might want to invest in an imported Japanese variety or two—there's even a low-sodium version available.

SPICES are often from stems, seeds, or roots of plants or trees, unlike herbs which are generally the leafy part of the plant.

Black Pepper is a crucial seasoning. Black peppercorns and a grinder are highly recommended. If you're not ready to make this investment, coarsely ground pepper comes already cracked and often offers far more texture and flavor compared to the superfine shaker version; it is available in most markets.

Cayenne Pepper This pungent, zestful spice is made from a blend of small ripe chilies—the heat is from cayenne chilies. Buy the ground variety, usually labeled "ground red pepper." A great pick-me-up for egg or cheese dishes.

Chili Powder is a seasoning common to many Mexican and Southwestern dishes. Chili powder is a mixture of dried ground chilies, cumin, cloves, coriander, garlic, and sometimes other herbs and spices.

Cinnamon is the spice of choice for many desserts, particularly those that include pears or apples. This is best bought in its ground form, as anyone who's tried to grate a cinnamon stick can tell you.

Cumin comes in both ground and dried whole-seed forms and is often used in Middle Eastern, Indian, and African dishes as well as in beans, dips, and chilies. It's also great over shellfish.

Curry Powder Common to many Indian dishes, this is a blend of many different seasonings (such as cardamon seeds, coriander seeds, black peppercorns, cumin, cloves, nutmeg) and varies from region to region. Curry can often turn a plain dish into something quite exotic.

Nutmeg It's worthwhile to buy the whole nut of this spice and grate it as needed into desserts, cream-based dishes, and slightly sweet savories, such as yams or beets. Invest in a nutmeg grater, if possible.

Paprika This ground spice of dried red sweet capsicum peppers loses its flavor quickly if not tightly lidded. Hungarian paprika is the most flavorful, but any variety can be used to perk up salad dressings and dips, potato and egg salads, and fish, poultry, and meat leftover improvisations.

Red Pepper Flakes can spice up even the blandest of foods. Use sparingly, tasting as you go. Not just for pizza.

TORTILLAS aren't just for burritos and enchiladas anymore, and can be recycled by cutting them into triangular shapes and baked into corn chips for dips or spreads (see page 20). Store them in the refrigerator, tightly wrapped, for one to two weeks. To soften them, sprinkle them with water and heat in the microwave.

VINEGAR is an indispensable kitchen staple. The most common varieties are rice, red, and white wine, plus malt and cider. Owning a good bottle of balsamic vinegar will allow you to perk up just about any food, particularly dressings and sauces.

THE
basics

1 Bagel Crisps

The '90s answer to "Day-Old Bread." Thinly slice those extra day-old bagels that may have lost their bakery freshness, then sprinkle on any of your favorite seasonings.

> *4 bagels*
> *2 teaspoons freshly grated parmesan cheese or 1 teaspoon dried herbs (such as oregano, parsley, rosemary, basil, or dill) or $1/2$ teaspoon cayenne pepper*

Preheat the broiler.

Thinly slice each bagel into four $1/4$-inch thick slices. Sprinkle the tops with generous amounts of the seasoning of your choice.

Arrange the bagels on a baking sheet in a single layer and toast for about 2 to 3 minutes, or until crispy. Serve hot or at room temperature.

2 Champagne Salad Dressing

How many times have you let that half bottle of fine French champagne gurgle down the drain because you know it will be flat by tomorrow's cocktail hour? This is truly a case of viewing the situation as not half empty but half full.

> *$1/2$ cup vegetable oil*
> *$1/4$ cup champagne*
> *1 teaspoon chopped fresh dill or tarragon*
> *pinch of salt*
> *freshly ground pepper*

In a small bowl, whisk together all the ingredients until emulsified.

Serve immediately over a green salad.

🥄 *Makes $3/4$ cup*

3 Champagne Sauce for Fish, Chicken, or Vegetables

Once it's heated, champagne always loses its fizz, so it won't matter that you are using "passive" champagne. In this sauce the sweet flavor of the champagne is most important. This is great over broiled mushrooms.

¹/₄ cup (¹/₂ stick) unsalted butter

4 tablespoons all-purpose flour

1 cup champagne

pinch of salt

¹/₂ teaspoon dried tarragon (optional)

In a skillet, cook the butter over low heat just until melted.

In small additions, gradually sift the flour over the melted butter, whisking after each addition until it is all incorporated and well blended. Remove the pan from the heat and gradually whisk in the champagne and add a pinch of salt.

Serve immediately over fish, chicken, pork, or vegetables. The sauce may be gently reheated over low heat and can be prepared ahead and stored in the refrigerator for up to three days, tightly wrapped.

🍳 *Makes about 1 cup*

4 Fish, Beef, Chicken, or Vegetable Stock

Stock is the essence of leftovers. Unwanted kitchen scraps and trimmings from expensive fish or chicken parts can be frozen and saved for making a healthy low-fat cooking staple.

FOR VEGETABLE STOCK

3 quarts cold water

1¼ pounds assorted cut-up fresh vegetables, such as carrots, turnips, parsnips, fennel, celery, or leeks

1 bay leaf

1 large yellow onion, peeled and cut in chunks

1 teaspoon black peppercorns

2 cloves garlic, peeled and crushed

4 tablespoons dried parsley

In a large stockpot (hence the name) combine all the ingredients. Bring to a boil over high heat, then reduce the heat to medium-low and let simmer for about 1 hour 15 minutes, skimming the surface occasionally with a large spoon.

Allow the stock to cool, then strain the stock through a fine-mesh strainer, using the back of a large spoon to press the cooked solids to extract any excess liquid.

Discard the cooked vegetables.

Temporarily place the stock in a large container, preferably one with a large surface area, and chill for 30 minutes.

Pour the stock into airtight containers of various sizes. Refrigerate the stock that will be used within 2 days and freeze the rest. ➤

19

FOR BEEF, CHICKEN, OR FISH

3 quarts cold water

1¹/₂ pounds beef, chicken, or fish (meat, skin, and bones)

1 bay leaf

1 large yellow onion, peeled and cut in chunks

1 teaspoon black peppercorns

2 cups assorted cut-up fresh vegetables, such as carrots, turnips, parsnips, fennel, celery, or leeks

2 cloves garlic, peeled and crushed

4 tablespoons dried parsley

Follow the instructions on page 19 for making vegetable stock, only this time skim the stock of any congealed fat after the initial refrigeration but before it is divided and stored.

🥄 *Makes about 2¹/₂ quarts*

5 Flavored Tortilla Chips

These are the ubiquitous chips that appear on the bar next to the salsa, only this time they are spiced up with the addition of some cayenne or another seasoning of your choice. Another advantage to making your own chips is that they are broiled, not fried, cutting back on unwanted fat, calories, and guilt.

6 leftover corn tortillas

vegetable oil

seasonings such as cumin, cayenne pepper, chili powder mixed with dried oregano, fresh herbs, or parmesan cheese

salt

Preheat the broiler.

Cut each tortilla into 6 to 8 chip-size wedges.

Place the chips on one or more baking sheets and brush lightly with oil. Sprinkle your favorite seasonings on the chips.

Place the tray(s) on the middle rack of the oven until the tortilla chips are curled and crisp.

Serve immediately with Salsa (see page 24), if desired.

🍳 *Makes about 3 cups*

6 Spicy Peanut Dip

Here's what to do with that half jar of PB long after you've run out of Saltines or Ritz crackers. Just fold in a few spicy ingredients and serve as a dip with apple slices, celery sticks, or anything else from skewered chicken to blanched broccoli. You can also toss this with hot cooked pasta for that great Chinese restaurant–style fave.

1 cup peanut butter, smooth or crunchy
2 scallions, green part only, finely chopped
1 jalapeño pepper, seeded and finely chopped
1 teaspoon minced fresh ginger
3 tablespoons vegetable or peanut oil
1 tablespoon sesame oil
2 tablespoons soy sauce
1 teaspoon minced garlic
1/4 teaspoon dried red pepper flakes
1 tablespoon honey

In a small bowl, blend all the ingredients. Chill, covered, for at least 1 hour. Refrigerate for up to 1 week, tightly covered.

🍳 *Makes about 1 generous cup*

7 All-Purpose Mayonnaise

Utilizing familiar ingredients found by rooting through your kitchen cabinets, this mayonnaise may be formulated for a myriad of savory dishes. Almost any leftover seasoning can be added to this to make a very personal condiment.

1 large egg

pinch of salt

$1/2$ teaspoon freshly squeezed lemon juice

1 cup extra-virgin olive oil

1 teaspoon additional seasonings, such as mixed fresh or dried herbs; roast garlic, shallots, or onion; finely chopped hot peppers, chopped gherkins, or capers

In a food processor or blender, add the egg, salt, lemon juice, and 1 teaspoon of the oil. Pulse once. With the motor running, in as slow a stream as possible, slowly drizzle in the oil through the opening.

The mixture will emulsify before your very eyes, but this takes patience and may take up to 5 full minutes. Only enough oil should be added to reach the desired consistency. This should not resemble store-bought mayonnaise, but should be yellower (or greener, depending upon the oil) and a bit looser.

Fold in the seasonings and chill for at least 2 hours. Store in the refrigerator in a tightly covered container for up to 4 days.

Makes about 1 cup

8 Herbed Butter, Margarine, or Cream Cheese

A fine example of emergency cuisine that works like clean underwear in a car wreck. Use this butter anytime you need to doctor up anything from poached chicken to steamed vegetables.

1/2 cup (1 stick) butter, margarine, or
4 ounces cream cheese, softened
1 teaspoon dried or 2 1/2 teaspoons fresh
chopped thyme, oregano, rosemary,
parsley, or any combination thereof
1/2 teaspoon grated lemon zest (optional)
salt and freshly ground pepper

In a small bowl, combine the butter, herbs, and lemon zest, if using. Season with salt and pepper and mix until well blended.

Roll into a log 1 inch in diameter, then wrap in plastic wrap. Chill until firm, about 45 minutes to an hour.

Serve as you would butter, or melt and brush the mixture on poultry or fish before baking.

This flavorful butter may be stored in the freezer for up to 3 weeks, or refrigerated, tightly covered, for 1 week.

Makes 1/2 cup

VARIATION: Berry Butter
Omit the herbs and salt and pepper, include the lemon zest, and add a few leftover ripe berries and a bit of sugar.

9 Guacamole

Just because an avocado is soft to the touch doesn't necessarily mean it's bad. Some of the best guacamoles are made from soft or over-ripe avocados. So before you toss out those soft or overripe avocados, try peeling the skin away and salvaging what isn't bruised or browned.

2 ripe Haas avocados (the best variety),
    peeled and pitted
1 ripe tomato, peeled, seeded, and diced
1 jalapeño pepper, finely chopped
1 tablespoon freshly chopped cilantro
2 teaspoons freshly squeezed lemon juice
salt and freshly ground pepper
Tabasco sauce to taste

In a large bowl, mash the avocados with the back of a fork until chunky. Gently blend in the remaining ingredients and chill, tightly covered, for at least 1 hour. Serve as a dip with crisp Flavored Tortilla Chips (see page 20), or alongside Mexican or Tex-Mex dishes. *Makes about 2 cups*

10 Black Bean and Corn Salsa

An impressive showing as salsas go, and remember homemade salsa says you care enough to ignore the far less delicious store-bought version. Serve this with your own homemade Flavored Tortilla Chips.

1¹/₂ cups (one 12-ounce can) cooked black
    beans, rinsed and drained

one 16-ounce can whole tomatoes, chopped
and drained
1 small yellow onion, peeled and chopped
³/₄ cup frozen corn kernels, cooked according to package directions
1 jalapeño pepper, finely minced
¹/₄ teaspoon cayenne pepper
2¹/₂ tablespoons chopped fresh cilantro
1 teaspoon chili powder
salt and freshly ground pepper

In a large bowl, mix all the ingredients until well blended.

Chill, covered, for at least 1 hour.

 *Makes 4 cups*

VARIATION: Substitute other kinds of beans, such as kidney, navy, or a combination for a more colorful blend.

I Love Olives

Leftover black olives can be drained, drizzled with extra-virgin olive oil, then dusted with a few dried red pepper flakes or some fresh or dried rosemary or thyme, or a few tablespoons of chopped fennel and a bit of minced garlic and served with cocktails. Leftover green olives can be tossed in some olive oil and sprinkled with fresh or dried rosemary leaves and a grind of coarse black pepper. Experiment with your favorite herbs and seasonings to create your own olives.

veget

We often buy vegetables in mas- sive quantities with all the best of intentions, either as the intended staple of a healthy diet or because they are better priced in bulk. Unfortunately, our good intentions often can't keep up with the evolution of time, and the veggies often become compost fare. Some leafier members of the vegetable family don't

ables

freeze particularly well, losing color, texture, and most important, flavor. However, some sturdier vegetables like carrots, turnips, leeks, onions, garlic, fennel, and parsnips are perfect to freeze for a future stock. A great tip is to keep a bag in your freezer to collect all those loose vegetable scraps, and once the bag is full you have the makings of a very flavorful broth (see page 19).

11 Caramelized Onion and Walnut Relish

Here is a delicious and practical use for the half-used bag of onions that's starting to resemble a thriving houseplant rather than a useful ingredient. It's a savory accompaniment to that massive rib roast or with steak and potatoes and is served with great frequency during the holidays.

1/4 cup (1/2 stick) unsalted butter

2 tablespoons sugar

2 medium yellow or Vidalia onions, peeled and sliced

4 tablespoons Beef, Chicken, or Vegetable Stock (see page 19)

1 cup whole shelled walnuts

salt and freshly ground pepper

In a large skillet, melt the butter and sugar over medium heat. Add the onions and cook, uncovered, stirring occasionally, until the onions are just soft and translucent, about 5 minutes.

Add the stock and simmer for 5 minutes more, then add the walnuts and cook for another 10 minutes, until most of the liquid has been absorbed. Season to taste with salt and pepper and serve immediately.

Makes 1 cup

12 Savory Sweet Potato Muffins with Red Peppers, Onion, and Bacon

Cakes, biscuits, muffins, and breads are perhaps the most practical and most successful way to use up a variety of ingredients at one time with delicious results. It's important to note this recipe, like most in this book, isn't meant to be followed with nunlike discipline. Just because you currently may be out of one of the many ingredients doesn't mean you can't be creative and improvise.

These muffins are great simply served with cold beer and a wedge of cheese. Of course, cold beer and a wedge of cheese are pretty fine on their own.

1 cup all-purpose flour
$1/2$ cup yellow cornmeal
1 tablespoon baking powder
2 tablespoons sugar
1 teaspoon salt
3 large eggs
$1/2$ cup milk
2 cups mashed sweet potatoes or yams
1 red or green pepper, stemmed, seeded, and diced
1 small onion, finely chopped
$1/2$ cup crumbled, cooked, and well-drained bacon
$1/4$ teaspoon dried red pepper flakes
2 teaspoons dried parsley
splash of Tabasco sauce (optional)
freshly ground pepper ➤

29

Preheat the oven to 400° F.

Line a total of 18 muffin cups with paper bake cups, or grease the muffin tin(s) well.

In a large bowl, sift together the flour, cornmeal, baking powder, sugar, and salt.

In another bowl beat the eggs until light. Add the milk and sweet potatoes and continue to stir until smooth. Then fold in the peppers, onion, bacon, red pepper flakes, parsley, and Tabasco sauce, and ground pepper.

Fold the wet ingredients into the dry just until blended.

Divide the batter evenly among the muffin cups, filling each about 2/3 full.

Bake in the middle rack of the oven for 20 to 25 minutes, or until a knife inserted in the center comes out clean.

Turn the muffins out onto a rack to cool.

☙ *Makes 18 muffins*

13 Low-Fat Potato Chips That Don't Taste Like Cardboard

The absence of oil or shortening makes these chips the friendliest alternative to the salty, oil-soaked chips we have come to love. And we thought they wouldn't taste good without all those delicious toxins and saturated fats!

2 Idaho or russet potatoes, scrubbed and sliced to 1/8 inch thickness

Preheat the oven to 350° F.

Place the potato slices directly on the oven rack or line the rack with aluminum foil first

30

and bake until golden brown and crispy, about 8 to 10 minutes.

Serve warm with malt vinegar, salt and pepper, or sprinkled with freshly grated cheese, herbs, paprika, cayenne, cumin, and on and on.

🍳 *Makes 2 cups*

14 Palma's Peach and Tomato Salad

An original composition of ingredients, perhaps a risk many of us are not confident enough to take, but remember, like the peach and eggplant, the tomato is technically a fruit.

This salad is a great accompaniment to grilled chicken or fish or as a light summer lunch.

> *3 tablespoons extra-virgin olive oil*
> *1 tablespoon freshly squeezed lemon juice*
> *3 ripe tomatoes, sliced and seeded*
> *2 ripe peaches, peeled, pitted, and sliced*
> *1/2 cup walnut halves*
> *coarsely ground pepper*

In a large bowl, whisk together the olive oil and lemon juice until combined.

Add the remaining ingredients and toss to coat evenly.

Chill, covered, for 1 hour.

🍳 *Serves 4*

15 The Simplest Ratatouille

This recipe is exceptionally handy when that gardening fetishist next door shows up at your house late in the summer bearing gifts of mutant zucchini that outweigh your dog.

If the task of all this chopping seems too arduous, just chop the ingredients separately in the food processor.

1 small eggplant, cut into ³/₄-inch chunks
salt
2 tablespoons extra-virgin olive oil
1 clove garlic, finely minced
1 medium yellow onion, chopped
2 large zucchini, cut into ³/₄-inch chunks
1 bell pepper, cored, seeded, and diced
one 12-ounce can whole tomatoes, coarsely chopped, with juice reserved
¹/₂ cup pitted black olives, sliced
1 cup dried bread crumbs
1 teaspoon dried thyme
1 teaspoon dried oregano
freshly ground pepper
¹/₂ cup grated parmesan cheese

Preheat the oven to 325° F.

Place the eggplant in a colander, sprinkle with salt, and let stand for 30 minutes. Then rinse and pat dry with paper towels.

In a deep pan over medium-high heat, add the oil and garlic and cook for 2 minutes. Add the onion and cook for another 4 minutes.

Add the eggplant and cook for another 5 minutes. Stir in the zucchini and pepper and continue to cook until all the ingredients are soft but not browned, about 7 minutes. Mix in the tomatoes and olives until well blended. Pour the mixture into a 9 × 13-inch baking pan.

In a separate bowl, combine the bread crumbs, herbs, and parmesan and stir well.

Top the ratatouille evenly with the bread-crumb mixture and bake for 35 to 40 minutes, or until the top is golden.

Let stand for 5 minutes before serving.

🥄 *Serves 4 to 6*

16 Mashed Potato Pancakes

Be they instant or homemade, mashed potatoes are most often made in excess. Leftover mashed potatoes can be used to make potato pancakes, or baked as a top crust for pot pies and stews. These pancakes are a great serving medium for all those smoked oysters, caviars, and salmon roe that find their way into your home via overwhelming holiday baskets of gourmet fruits, cheeses, and other goodies.

4 cups mashed potatoes
2 large eggs, lightly beaten
$1/4$ cup heavy cream
2 scallions, finely minced
1 teaspoon dried parsley or
* $2^1/_2$ teaspoons fresh chopped parsley*
1 cup all-purpose flour
1 teaspoon baking powder
$1/4$ teaspoon salt
freshly ground pepper
vegetable oil for frying

In a large bowl, fold the potatoes together with the eggs, cream, scallions, parsley, flour, ➤

baking powder, and salt and pepper until well combined.

Cover and chill the mixture for 1 hour.

In a large skillet, heat $1/4$ inch oil over medium heat.

By tablespoonfuls drop the mixture into the oil and cook for 5 minutes on each side, or until crispy.

Drain the potato pancakes on paper towels and keep them warm in a 200° F. oven until all are cooked.

Serve immediately with sour cream and caviar, applesauce, or just salt and pepper.

☞ *Makes about 18 pancakes*

VARIATION: Sweet Potato Pancakes
You can substitute mashed sweet potatoes for part or all of the regular mashed potatoes.

17 Marinated Summer Vegetable Salad

Before you grace the top of your compost heap with those unused summer vegetables, you might want to give them another chance. Giant homegrown vegetables don't have to just sit around and be admired like gardening trophies until they go bad. They can achieve more lasting beauty by being pickled or becoming part of this simple dish that goes as well with sandwiches as it does with steak and potatoes. It's also a fine hors d'oeuvre, especially accompanying a bowl of olives, an array of cheeses, and some good crusty bread.

$^1/_8$ cup extra-virgin olive oil

3 tablespoons balsamic vinegar

1 teaspoon dried herbs (such as a mixture
   of oregano and basil) or $2^1/_2$ teaspoons
   fresh chopped herbs

salt and freshly ground pepper

3 cups blanched vegetables, such as string
   beans, zucchini, cauliflower, etc., cut
   into bite-size pieces

$^1/_2$ teaspoon capers

$^1/_2$ cup pine nuts, walnut halves, or toasted
   slivered almonds (optional)

In a large bowl, mix together the olive oil, vinegar, herbs, salt and pepper.

Add the cooked vegetables and capers (plus the nuts, if you're using them) and stir to coat.

Chill, covered, for at least 1 hour, tossing occasionally. Correct seasonings and serve.

🍂 *Makes about 3 cups*

Peanuts Envy

Plain nuts are fine, but throw in a seasoning or two and they become superior snacking. In a large bowl combine 2 tablespoons melted butter, $^1/_8$ teaspoon cinnamon or a pinch of nutmeg, 1 tablespoon sugar, a pinch of salt, and 1 cup of leftover unsalted peanuts or mixed nuts. Toss until well coated. Toast in a single layer on a baking sheet under a preheated broiler for about 5 minutes, or until browned, stirring once or twice. Let cool and serve in a bowl.

18 Baked Cherry Tomatoes and Couscous

Cherry tomatoes, like relatives, often come in numbers too great to accommodate in one sitting. This dish will not only serve the masses but gracefully use up all of those tomatoes in an inexpensive couscous before it's too late.

butter for greasing the baking dish
1 pound fresh cherry tomatoes, washed
    well
2 cups cooked couscous (prepared according to package directions)
1 clove fresh garlic, chopped
¼ cup chopped fresh parsley
1 teaspoon chopped fresh thyme leaves or
    ½ teaspoon dried thyme
¼ cup grated parmesan, romano, or
    Asiago cheese
salt and freshly ground pepper

Butter a 6 × 10-inch baking pan or oven-proof dish.

Preheat the oven to 400° F.

Arrange the tomatoes in a single layer in the prepared pan.

In a large bowl, mix together the couscous, garlic, parsley, thyme, and cheese of choice.

Evenly spread the couscous mixture over the tomatoes and season to taste with salt and pepper.

Cover the pan with foil and bake on the middle rack of the oven for 30 minutes, then uncover and bake for 5 minutes more.

Let stand for 7 to 10 minutes, then serve.

🍳 *Serves 6*

19 Very Basic Baked Potato Skins

Singles' bar cuisine, only homemade and you don't need a date. Leftover baked potatoes have a multitude of uses. The pulp of the left-over potatoes can be used for everything from thickening soups and gravies, to toppings for stews and pot pies, and the skins can be topped with any selection of cheeses or seasonings, then broiled and served as a snack or hors d'oeuvres.

4 baked potatoes
1/2 cup shredded cheddar or Monterey Jack cheese
1 teaspoon finely minced jalapeño pepper, or to taste
salt and freshly ground pepper
Black Bean and Corn Salsa or Guacamole to serve (optional, see page 24)

Preheat the oven to 400° F.

Cut the potatoes in half lengthwise.

Scoop out the potatoes and reserve the insides for another use (of which there are many—see page 33, for example).

Arrange the potato halves on a baking sheet or in an ovenproof dish.

Sprinkle the cheese and chopped jalapeño over the potato skins.

Season to taste with salt and pepper.

Bake for 10 to 15 minutes, or until the cheese is golden and bubbly.

Serve immediately with homemade Black Bean and Corn Salsa or Guacamole, if desired.

☙ *Makes 8 potato skins*

20 Vegetable-Bin Gazpacho

This multi-ingredient soup is a great way to free up some of that lost space in the vegetable drawer of your refrigerator. I like this soup on the chunky side, but to make it smoother, pureé half the mixture in the blender before serving.

4 large tomatoes, cored, chopped, and seeded

1 cucumber, peeled, seeded, and diced

1 green or red bell pepper, stemmed, seeded, and diced

1 medium yellow onion, finely chopped

1 clove garlic, finely minced

2 tablespoons red wine vinegar

splash of Tabasco sauce

3 cups tomato juice

salt and freshly ground pepper

plain yogurt or sprigs of Italian parsley for garnish

In a large bowl, combine all the ingredients and chill for at least 1 hour.

Serve in bowls or mugs, garnished with a dollop of plain yogurt or sprigs of parsley.

🥄 *Makes 6 cups*

21 Steamed Dumplings

Like covering foods in melted cheese, anything flies once encased inside a pie crust, wonton, or tortilla. These savories can also be fried and shamelessly served under the alias of "Beggar's Purses" as an hors d'oeuvre.

1 teaspoon vegetable oil

1 clove garlic, finely minced

1 scallion, chopped

1/2 teaspoon chopped fresh ginger

1/4 cup chicken or vegetable stock

1 cup cooked chicken, shrimp, or
*   vegetables, such as broccoli, carrots,*
*   leeks, or spinach, finely chopped*

1/4 teaspoon dried red pepper flakes

18 wonton skins

SIMPLE DIPPING SAUCE

6 tablespoons rice wine vinegar

2 teaspoons white vinegar

red pepper flakes or chopped scallion
*   to taste*

In a large skillet over medium heat, heat the oil, then add the garlic and scallion and cook for 3 to 4 minutes, until softened. Add the ginger and continue to cook for another 3 to 4 minutes.

Add the stock to the scallion mixture and bring to a simmer. Add the chicken, shrimp, or vegetables and continue to cook until the mixture is heated through and almost all the stock has been absorbed. Add the red pepper flakes and remove the mixture from the heat and allow to cool.

Place about 1 teaspoon of the mixture in the middle of each wonton skin. Brush the dough edges with water, fold the wonton in half, and press to tightly seal.

In a large saucepan, bring 3/4 inch of water to a boil over medium-high heat.

Oil the inside of a steamer insert or basket.

Steam the dumplings in a single layer over rapidly boiling water for about 8 minutes, or until they are soft and pale.

Serve immediately with the Simple Dipping Sauce, hot chili oil, or soy sauce.

Makes 18 dumplings

39

22 Chili Roasted Corn

Here it's important to use leftover ears of cooked fresh corn, as the texture and flavor differs so completely from its often soggy canned or creamed counterparts.

1 small onion, coarsely chopped
1 jalapeño pepper, seeded and diced
2 tablespoons melted unsalted butter
1 teaspoon chili powder
1/2 teaspoon ground cumin
salt and freshly ground pepper
2 cups corn kernels, cut from the ears fresh
of steamed or boiled corn

Preheat the broiler.

In a large bowl, combine the onion, jalapeño, butter, chili powder, cumin, and salt and pepper. Add the corn and toss well to coat.

Place the mixture in a single layer on an ungreased baking sheet. Broil for about 5 minutes, then stir and broil for another 5 minutes, or until the corn is evenly browned.

Serve immediately.

Makes about 2 1/2 cups

23 Haven't-I-Seen-You-Before Vegetable Tart

I often wonder why things like ricotta cheese and plain yogurt most often come in portions too big to use in a reasonable amount of time.

Before you know it the container you forgot in your fridge a week ago is now glowing with mold. This tart is also a great remedy for those leftover steamed vegetables.

1 cup ricotta cheese
1/2 cup plain nonfat yogurt
one 10-ounce package frozen spinach, thawed
1/2 teaspoon ground nutmeg
salt and freshly ground pepper
1 small onion or 1 shallot, finely chopped
one 9-inch unbaked pie crust (store-bought is fine)
2 cups mixed chopped fresh vegetables, such as zucchini, eggplant, summer squash, cauliflower, etc.
1 cup shredded mozzarella or Gruyère, or 1/2 cup crumbled goat cheese
fresh herbs for garnish

Preheat the oven to 400° F.

Line a strainer with cheesecloth or a coffee filter and place over a large bowl. Combine the ricotta and yogurt in the strainer. Put the bowl in the refrigerator and allow it to drain for at least 2 hours (overnight is preferable). Discard the liquid.

Squeeze all the liquid from the spinach. In a large bowl blend the spinach and ricotta mixture. Blend in the nutmeg, salt, pepper, and chopped onion or shallot.

Spread this mixture evenly over the pie crust.

Arrange the mixed vegetables on top.

Top evenly with the cheese and bake for 45 minutes, or until the top is golden and bubbly.

Let stand for 10 minutes before serving. Cut into wedges and garnish with fresh herbs to serve.

Makes one 9-inch pie

Green *by design*

INTENTIONALLY GREEN	SHOULD NOT BE GREEN
most lettuce	chili
string beans	cheese
celery	almost all Chinese food
jalapeños	all meat
zucchini	coconut flakes
basil	sour cream
artichokes	fish sticks
limes	bread
avocados	cold cuts
peas	the dairy family
pickles	raspberries
brussel sprouts	spaghetti

24 Vegetable and Feta Cheese Soufflé

Soufflés are always a success once you realize that they are supposed to fall. It's the change in temperature that occurs as they are cooling that forces them inevitably to collapse. The trick is to serve them up as quickly as possible. And hey, if it falls, it falls.

butter and flour to prepare ramekin dishes
2 cups cooked vegetables, such as zucchini,
summer squash, fennel, leek, spinach,
daikon, etc., shredded or cut into
1/8-inch julienne strips
salt

3 tablespoons unsalted butter or margarine

1/4 cup all-purpose flour

1/4 teaspoon dry mustard

1 cup milk

1/2 cup crumbled feta or Gorgonzola cheese

1 tablespoon freshly grated parmesan or
   Asiago cheese

4 large eggs, separated

Preheat the oven to 375° F.

Butter and flour six 6-ounce ramekins or custard cups.

Place the shredded vegetables in a colander, sprinkle with salt, and toss lightly. Let stand for 30 minutes. Rinse and squeeze out the excess liquid. Set aside.

In a large saucepan over medium heat, melt the butter. Stir in the flour and dry mustard and whisk until smooth. Add the milk. Continue to cook until bubbly. Remove from the heat and stir in the vegetables and cheese until well blended, about 4 minutes.

In a large bowl, beat the egg yolks with a fork. Fold in the vegetable mixture.

In a separate bowl, with a hand mixer or whisk, beat the egg whites until stiff peaks form. Gently fold the whites into the vegetable mixture in three additions. Carefully pour the mixture evenly into the ramekins.

Bake for 20 to 25 minutes, or until a knife inserted in the center comes out clean.

Serve immediately.

Makes 6 servings

43

25 Onion Tart
(Basically a Quiche)

This picks up where Lorraine left off.

1 pound small yellow onions (about 7 or 8)

1 cup Chicken or Vegetable Stock (use homemade, page 19, if available)

2 large eggs

1/4 cup ricotta cheese

1/4 cup sour cream

1/4 cup grated parmesan cheese

1/4 cup sherry

1 clove garlic, minced

salt and freshly ground pepper

one 9-inch unbaked pie shell (store-bought is fine)

Preheat the oven to 375° F.

Peel the onions, removing any roots or stems, but leaving them intact.

In a large saucepan over medium heat, bring the stock to a gentle simmer. Add the onions in a single layer and cook for about 10 minutes, or until they can be pierced easily with a fork. Using a slotted spoon, remove the onions to layered paper towels to drain and cool. Discard the remaining stock.

In a large bowl, beat the eggs and fold in the ricotta, sour cream, and parmesan. Add the sherry, garlic, and salt and pepper to taste.

When the onions are cool, slice each of them once through the middle crosswise and arrange them cut-side down in a single layer in the pie crust. Pour the batter evenly over the onions.

Bake on the middle rack of the oven for 35 to 40 minutes or until the filling is golden and the crust is brown. Let stand for 10 minutes. Cut into wedges and serve.

Makes one 9-inch pie

26 Nondairy Cream of Vegetable Soup

This is cuisine with the diet-conscious or lactose-intolerant in mind. Here the "Cream of" comes not from milk or cream but from the potato. Ironically, this soup is even better after it has cooled and been reheated: second-generation leftovers.

1 tablespoon extra-virgin olive oil
1 clove garlic, minced
2 cups mashed potatoes
1 cup Chicken or Vegetable Stock (use homemade, page 19, if possible)
2 cups cooked vegetables, such as broccoli, cauliflower, carrots, leeks, turnips, spinach, etc., finely chopped
1/4 teaspoon ground white pepper
salt
1 tablespoon fresh oregano, dill, or tarragon or 1 teaspoon dried herb
1 tablespoon fresh parsley or 1 teaspoon dried

In a large stockpot over medium heat, combine the oil and garlic and cook until the garlic has turned golden, about 2 minutes.

Stir in the mashed potatoes and gradually add the stock until the mixture is creamy and well blended. Stir in the cooked vegetables.

Blend in the remaining seasonings and reduce the heat to low. Let the soup simmer for about 15 minutes. Serve immediately.

Makes 4 cups

poultry, fish & meat

The recipes follow basically the same culinary principle or equation, and that is: Put anything inside a pie crust, on a pizza, encased in a tortilla, or wrapped in a wonton, serve it with your usual finesse, and call it dinner.

Average Lifespans

To avoid food-borne illness and maintain fresh-ness, flavor, and texture, keep your fridge at a temperature between 35° and 45° F. and your freezer at 0° F. The following wealth of information was obtained by calling the U.S. Department of Agriculture's Food Safety Hotline.

FROZEN FOODS SHOULD BE USED IN:

Whole chicken or turkey, beef roasts, and steaks	1 year
Poultry parts, lamb roasts, and chops	9 months
Pork and veal chops	6 months
Ground meats, organ meats	4 months
Leftovers and cooked foods	3 months
Canned ham, unopened packages of bacon, sausage, lunch meats, and hot dogs	2 months

REFRIGERATOR LIFE OF FOODS:

Fresh cuts of beef and pork	3 to 5 days
Ground beef, stew meats, chicken, organ meats, and fresh sausage	1 to 2 days
Eggs	2 to 3 weeks
Cooked foods and leftovers, cooked meat, soup, and stew	3 to 4 days
Fully cooked hams, lunch meats from the deli and opened packages	3 to 5 days
Open packages of hot dogs, bacon, and hard-cooked eggs	1 week
Unopened canned ham	9 months
Dried sausages, unopened packages of lunch meats and hot dogs	2 weeks
Never leave perishable foods out of the refrigerator for more than	2 hours

Thawing is best accomplished in the refrigerator with foods in their original wrapping

27 A Very Humble Pot Pie

Rather than subject yourself to another maternal chorus of "If you don't eat it, I'll just throw it away!" why not reinvent those sometimes unfamiliar table scraps into an American Standard. This recipe is especially tasty when wine is substituted for the requisite stock to make the gravy.

1/2 package frozen puff pastry (1 sheet)
butter and flour to prepare pie plate
3 tablespoons sweet butter
1 medium yellow onion, coarsely chopped
1 cup sliced white mushrooms
2 tablespoons all-purpose flour
1 cup chicken stock or white wine

2 cups cooked chicken, turkey, or pork, cubed
1/4 cup frozen peas
1/2 teaspoon dried parsley
1/2 teaspoon dried sage
salt and pepper to taste

Preheat the oven to 400° F.

Thaw the pastry according to the instructions given on the package.

Butter and flour one 8-inch pie plate.

In a large saucepan over a low-medium heat, melt 1 tablespoon of the butter.

Add the onion and cook just until translucent (about 5 minutes).

Stir in the mushrooms and cook for another 5 minutes or until the mushrooms are tender.

Remove the onions and mushrooms from the pan and reserve.

Reduce the heat and melt the remaining butter. Sift in the flour, stirring constantly

48

until the mixture is thick. Gradually stir in the chicken stock or wine and continue to stir until thick and well blended.

Fold in the chicken, turkey, or pork, and peas and stir until well coated.

Stir in the cooked onions and mushrooms and blend well.

Add the parsley and sage, salt and pepper.

Pour the mixture into the prepared pie plate and spread evenly.

If necessary, roll the pastry out on a well-floured surface to fit the top of the pie.

Place the pastry over the pie plate and crimp the edges. Trim away any excess pastry.

Bake for 25 to 30 minutes or until the pastry is puffed and golden.

Let stand on a wire rack for 5 to 10 minutes before serving.

☛ *Makes one 8-inch pie*

28 Deviled Ham Spread

The results of these ham recipes depends on the quality of the meat you use, and it works well with both baked and smoked versions. If the ham is packed in gelatin, discard the jelly.

> *4 cups cooked ham, cubed or julienned*
> *1/4 cup mayonnaise*
> *2 tablespoons smooth Dijon mustard*
> *2 tablespoons chopped gherkin pickles or 1 teaspoon chopped capers*
> *freshly ground black pepper*

Put the ham in a food processor and chop just until coarse.

Add the mayonnaise, mustard, pickles or capers, and continue processing until the ➤

mixture is well blended and fairly smooth. Season with pepper, cover the mixture tightly, and chill for at least 1 hour.

Serve on sandwich bread with sliced fresh cucumber, or on crackers as an hors d'oeuvre. This spread should last for 3 to 5 days in the refrigerator, if tightly covered.

🍳 *Makes 3 cups*

29 Hash of Red Snapper or Corned Beef

Simply served on toast with just a poached egg, hash is a great way to feed a large number of people with little effort and small amounts of leftover food. A far cry from the canned version, this flavorful mixture will convert the most adamant hash skeptic.

> *1/4 cup (1/2 stick) unsalted butter*
> *1 clove garlic, minced*
> *1 Idaho or russet potato, scrubbed and diced*
> *1 medium yellow onion, chopped*
> *1 stalk celery, diced*
> *1/2 green or red pepper, stemmed, seeded, and diced*
> *3 cups flaked cooked fish, any skin and bones removed*
> or
> *3 cups finely chopped or ground corned or roast beef*

FOR FISH
> *1/4 cup chopped fresh dill*
> *1 tablespoon freshly grated lemon zest*

¹/₄ cup chopped fresh parsley
salt and freshly ground black pepper

In a large skillet over medium heat melt the butter. Add the garlic and cook until golden and fragrant, about 1 minute. Stir in the potatoes and continue to cook for another 7 minutes, or until the potatoes have browned.

Add the onion, celery, and pepper, and continue to cook until all the ingredients are tender yet crispy, about 10 minutes.

Stir in the cooked fish or beef and continue to cook until all ingredients are piping hot.

Stir in the remaining ingredients, using whichever seasonings are appropriate, and season with salt and pepper to taste.

Serve over a bed of salad greens with lemon wedges, or on toast and topped with a poached egg.

🥄 *Makes 4 servings*

30 Vol-au-Vent

Just as Croque Monsieur is a fancy synonym for a Grilled Cheese Sandwich, Vol-au-Vent is just another snappy pseudonym for Creamed Chicken on Toast.

one 1-pound frozen puff-pastry shells
3 tablespoons unsalted butter
1 cup white wine
3 tablespoons all-purpose flour
1 teaspoon dried tarragon leaves or 2¹/₂
     teaspoons fresh tarragon
salt and freshly ground pepper
3 cups cooked cubed chicken

Bake the pastry shells according to the package instructions.

In a large skillet over medium heat, melt the butter. Gradually add both the wine and ➤

51

flour in three additions, whisking to blend, then add the tarragon and continue to whisk until thick and well blended, about 5 minutes. Season to taste with salt and pepper.

Stir in the chicken and mix until well coated.

With a slotted spoon, spoon the chicken evenly into the prepared pastry shells. Pour the remaining sauce evenly over the chicken.

Serve immediately.

🍳 *Makes 6 servings*

Things that *should* move in your fridge

SHOULD MOVE	SHOULD NOT MOVE
live lobsters	freshly cooked lobster
Jell-O	everything else

---

31 Anything in a Tortilla

Just like its name, anything goes when you use any or all of these great seasonings and ingredients. This recipe is a great one to play with to come up with your own signature burrito come leftover day.

1 tablespoon extra-virgin olive oil

1 clove garlic, finely minced

1 yellow onion, chopped

1 bell pepper, cored, seeded, and cut into $^1/_8$-inch julienne strips

1 jalapeño pepper, seeded and minced (optional)

$^1/_2$ teaspoon cumin

$^1/_2$ to 1 teaspoon chili powder

a few drops Tabasco sauce

1 teaspoon freshly squeezed lemon juice

cayenne pepper to taste

salt and freshly ground pepper

2 cups cooked cubed chicken, beef, or shrimp

4 large corn or flour tortillas

1/2 cup shredded cheddar or Monterey Jack cheese

fresh cilantro or lime wedges for garnish

Preheat the oven to 350° F.

In a large skillet, heat the oil over medium heat. Add the garlic and cook until lightly browned, about 2 minutes.

Add the onion and peppers and cook until the peppers are crisp-tender and the onions are tender and translucent, about 5 minutes. Add the jalapeño, cumin, chili powder, Tabasco sauce, lemon juice, cayenne, salt and pepper. Continue to cook for another minute.

Add the chicken, beef, or shrimp and stir just until all the ingredients are heated through.

Spoon 1/4 of the mixture in a line down the center of each tortilla. Carefully fold the ends of the tortillas in, then fold the remaining ends over each other.

Arrange the tortillas, folded side-down, on a baking sheet or ovenproof dish.

Evenly sprinkle the shredded cheese over the prepared tortillas and bake for about 20 minutes, or until the cheese is bubbly and golden.

Garnish with fresh cilantro or lime wedges.

Serve immediately.

Makes 4 burritos

32 Reprieve Fish Cakes

A delicious reprieve that would make even Mrs. Paul green with envy, these are most stylishly served with your own homemade All-Purpose Mayonnaise (see page 22) and a little chopped cornichon pickle. These little fritter-like cakes make great hors d'oeuvres.

1 lemon
1/2 cup milk
3 large eggs, lightly beaten
1/2 cup all-purpose flour
1/2 cup yellow cornmeal
1 teaspoon baking powder
1/2 teaspoon salt

1 1/2 cups cooked chopped firm-fleshed fish (such as salmon, tuna, swordfish, mahi mahi, grouper), or shellfish, such as crab or lobster
1 leek, white part only, or 1 stalk celery, cleaned and chopped
1 1/2 teaspoons curry powder
1/2 teaspoon ground ginger
freshly ground pepper
vegetable oil for frying

Zest the lemon, then squeeze the juice from it. Reserve the zest and the juice in two separate bowls.

In a large bowl, blend the milk and eggs.

In another bowl, sift together the flour, cornmeal, baking powder, and salt. Add the dry ingredients to the egg mixture and stir to combine. Add the fish, leek or celery, lemon zest, curry powder, ginger, and pepper. Blend until smooth.

In a large skillet, heat $1/4$ inch of oil over medium heat.

Drop batter by the tablespoon into the oil.

Cook for 5 minutes on each side, until golden and crispy. Don't flip the cakes until they have cooked completely on one side.

Remove the fish cakes with a slotted spoon to paper towels to drain.

Serve immediately.

🥄 *Makes 12 fish cakes*

33 Cayenne Fried Ham

A big baked ham can seem more like a guilt-inspiring albatross; you feel obligated to make use of it, but one can eat just so many ham sandwiches. Here's a spicy alternative to bacon, and one that's a lot leaner, too.

2 tablespoons unsalted butter

1 teaspoon sugar

$1/8$ teaspoon cayenne pepper, or to taste

$1/4$ pound baked ham, sliced to $1/4$-inch thickness

In a large skillet over a medium heat, melt the butter. Add the sugar and stir until the sugar has melted, then stir in the cayenne pepper.

Cook the ham slices as you would bacon, until they are browned and crisp, about 4 minutes on each side.

Remove the ham to paper towels and drain. Serve hot.

🥄 *Serves 2*

34 Post-Thanksgiving Curried Turkey Meat Loaf

With an overabundance of leftover turkey, this will provide you with another dinner, and possibly sandwiches the next day. A welcome respite from the culinary slings and arrows of dishes like Turkey Jell-O Salad Loaf or Marshmallow Turkey Fettuccine.

4 cups finely chopped or ground roast turkey (about 1 pound), both white and dark meat

1 medium yellow onion, chopped

2 cloves garlic, finely minced

2 cups dry bread crumbs

1/4 cup freshly chopped parsley

2 large eggs, lightly beaten

3/4 cup mayonnaise

1 teaspoon curry powder

1 teaspoon minced fresh ginger

1/2 teaspoon dry mustard

2 teaspoons grated lemon or orange zest

1/2 cup heavy cream or milk

1/4 teaspoon ground white pepper

2 tablespoons sesame seeds

Preheat the oven to 350° F.

In a large bowl, mix all the ingredients together (except for the sesame seeds) with clean hands until the mixture is well blended.

Press the mixture into an ungreased 8¹/₂ × 4¹/₂ × 2¹/₂-inch loaf pan.

Sprinkle the top with the sesame seeds and gently press them into the top.

Bake for 50 minutes to 1 hour, or until the top has browned.

Serve hot or at room temperature.

🍳 *Serves 4*

35 Revival of the Fittest "Stir-Fry"

A stir-fry is perhaps the easiest and most common way to repackage leftovers without the use of breading or crusts and, more important, without generating an abundance of dirty dishes. A wok or esoteric utensils are not required—all you need is a good skillet and a little imagination.➤

1 tablespoon vegetable oil

1 clove garlic, minced

1 medium onion, coarsely chopped

$1/2$ green or red pepper, stemmed, seeded
   and cut into 1-inch pieces

1 stalk celery, sliced crosswise

2 cups cooked, cubed chicken, beef,
   or shrimp

one 5-ounce can water chestnuts,
   drained

$1/2$ cup snow peas, stems removed and cut
   lengthwise into strips

4 tablespoons soy sauce

3 tablespoons sugar or honey

dash of hot chili oil

2 teaspoons freshly chopped cilantro

$1/4$ cup sesame seeds, toasted

1 cup pineapple chunks (optional)

1 cup baby corn ears (optional)

cooked white or brown rice to serve

In a large skillet over medium heat, heat the oil, then add the garlic and cook until golden and fragrant, about 2 minutes. Turn up the heat and add the onion, red pepper, and celery, and continue to cook until crisp-tender, about 4 minutes, stirring often.

Add the chicken, beef, or shrimp, the water chestnuts, and snow peas and continue to stir until heated through.

Add the soy sauce, sugar or honey, hot chili oil, and cilantro, and continue to cook until the sugar has melted and glazed the ingredients.

Toss in the sesame seeds and serve immediately over white or brown rice.

🍳 *Serves 4*

58

36 Catch of the Day Salade Niçoise

This Salade Niçoise is a delicious excuse to take liberties with a traditional recipe.

1/2 cup string beans or asparagus stalks, cut into 1-inch pieces

1 cup torn salad greens, such as romaine, endive, Boston, or baby lettuce

1 cup flaked, cooked, or grilled firm-fleshed fish (such as salmon or tuna)

1 hard-cooked egg, sliced

1/2 cup cooked small red or white potatoes, cut in quarters

2 teaspoons capers or chopped black olives

4 anchovy filets, rinsed, patted dry, and chopped

1/2 cup canned artichoke hearts, drained and halved

extra-virgin olive oil and balsamic vinegar

1/4 cup homemade All-Purpose Mayonnaise (see page 22)

Bring a saucepan of water to boil over a medium-high heat. Add the string beans or asparagus and blanch for 2 to 3 minutes, or until crisp-tender. Drain.

Line a bowl with the salad greens, then arrange the fish, egg, potatoes, capers, anchovies, and artichokes.

Drizzle with extra-virgin olive oil and a splash of balsamic or red wine vinegar or serve with a dollop of mayonnaise.

Serve immediately.

Serves 2

37 Cream of Yesterday Soup

This basic cream soup recipe will work easily with most vegetables, but make sure that they are well rinsed and allowed to dry thoroughly. Allow mushrooms to dry thoroughly as they "retain" a lot of water and this could result in a thinner, less flavorful soup.

2 tablespoons vegetable oil

2 cloves garlic, finely chopped

1 medium yellow onion, chopped

1 cup cooked chopped chicken, beef, or vegetables

2 tablespoons all-purpose flour

1 cup Chicken or Vegetable Stock (homemade, if available, see page 19)

1 teaspoon Dijon mustard

1 cup heavy cream or milk, at room temperature

¼ cup freshly chopped parsley

salt and freshly ground pepper

In a stockpot heat the oil over medium heat. Add the garlic and cook until fragrant and golden, about 2 minutes. Add the onion and continue to cook until the onion is translucent, about 5 minutes.

Increase the heat to medium-high and add the chicken, beef, or vegetables. Cook for another 5 minutes, stirring occasionally. Remove the aforementioned chicken, meat, or vegetables with a slotted spoon and reserve.

Reduce the heat to medium and whisk in 1 tablespoon of the flour with ¼ cup of the stock. Continue to whisk in the rest of the flour and stock, whisking until the mixture is free of any lumps and is bubbly. Add the

60

mustard and milk and continue to whisk until mixture has thickened slightly, about 5 minutes. Return the chicken, beef, or vegetables to the pot and let simmer for 20–30 minutes. Add the parsley and season to taste with salt and pepper. Serve hot.

🍳 *Makes 4 cups*

38 Tamale Pie

Anybody who has ever eaten a school cafeteria lunch will fondly remember casseroles and stews of this nature.

> *2 tablespoons unsalted butter*
> *1 clove garlic, finely minced*
> *1 large onion, chopped*
> *1 stalk celery, finely diced*

> *1 jalapeño or hot finger pepper, seeded and finely chopped*
> *one 28-ounce can whole tomatoes, chopped, juice reserved*
> *1 cup frozen corn kernels*
> *1½ tablespoons chili powder*
> *⅛ teaspoon cayenne pepper or ¼ teaspoon dried red pepper flakes, or to taste*
> *splash of Tabasco sauce (optional)*
> *4 cups chopped cooked chicken or beef*
> *salt and freshly ground pepper*
> *1 cup milk*
> *1 cup all-purpose flour*
> *1 cup coarsely ground yellow cornmeal*
> *one 4-ounce can chopped green chilies, drained*

Preheat the oven to 350° F.

Butter and flour an 11 × 7-inch baking dish. In a large skillet over medium heat, melt the butter. Add the garlic and cook just until➤

fragrant, about 1 minute. Add the onion, celery, and jalapeño and continue to cook until the onion is just translucent and the celery is wilting, about 5 minutes.

Stir in the tomatoes with their juice and let simmer for 5 minutes.

Blend in the corn, chili powder, cayenne, and Tabasco sauce (if desired), then add the beef or chicken and continue to stir until well blended. Add salt and pepper to taste.

In a large bowl, gradually add the milk, flour, and cornmeal, in three additions each, whisking until smooth.

Pour the chicken or beef mixture into the prepared baking dish. Evenly spread the cornmeal batter on top of that, then top with the chopped chilies.

Bake for 30 to 35 minutes, or until the top is crisp. Let stand for 5 minutes and serve hot.

Serves 4 to 6

39 The Inevitable Tetrazzini

Anyone who has browsed through his or her mother's old housekeeping magazines has probably been confronted with a number of tetrazzini recipes. Ultimately this is just meat, chicken, or turkey smothered under a bed of very creamy egg noodles and generously coated with commercial bread crumbs. It was very popular in the '60s, long before any effort at low-fat or low-calorie cuisine reared its dietary head. Here it's been reinvented with the addition of fresh wild mushrooms and chopped walnuts, and the removal of some fat—although not all of it, thank God.

3 tablespoons unsalted butter

1/2 pound fresh wild mushrooms (such as
    shiitake, portobello, cremini, oyster,
    porcini, or morel), washed, trimmed,
    and any tough stems removed

3 tablespoons all-purpose flour

1/2 cup heavy cream

1 cup white wine

3/4 cup freshly grated parmesan, romano,
    or Asiago cheese

3 cups cubed cooked turkey

3 cups cooked short pasta shapes, such as
    penne, rigatoni, rotini, or farfalle

1/8 teaspoon ground nutmeg

pinch of salt

1/2 cup dry bread crumbs

1/2 cup chopped walnuts

Preheat the oven to 375° F.

In a large saucepan over medium heat, melt the butter. Add the mushrooms and sauté for 5 minutes, or until they render their juices. Remove the mushrooms from the pan with a slotted spoon and reserve.

Reduce the heat to medium-low and gradually add the flour, cream, and 3/4 cup of the wine to the mushroom liquid whisking until the mixture is smooth and bubbly.

Blend in the cheese and continue stirring until the cheese melts. Add the rest of the wine and stir until smooth. Add the turkey, pasta, nutmeg, and salt and toss to coat.

Pour the mixture into a 13 × 9 × 2-inch baking dish. Top with the bread crumbs and chopped walnuts. Bake for 25 to 30 minutes, or until the top is golden.

Let stand for 5 minutes and serve hot.

Makes 6 servings

pasta, bread & rice

40 Chinese Rice Timbale

Although your leftover take-out rice has probably retained the inimitable obtuse shape of its original container, you might explore reshaping it in a slightly more inviting way and throwing in a few simple additions.

butter for greasing ramekins
2 cups cooked white or brown rice
$1/4$ cup sundried tomatoes (not oil-packed),
  coarsely chopped
$1/4$ cup peas, fresh or frozen
3 tablespoons pine nuts
1 shallot, minced
2 teaspoons fresh lemon juice
4 tablespoons freshly grated parmesan,
  romano, or Asiago cheese
$1/2$ teaspoon dried parsley or oregano
salad greens (such as butter lettuce, mâche,
  or radicchio) to serve

Preheat the oven to 350° F. Generously butter four 4-ounce ramekins or custard cups.

In a large bowl, mix the rice with the rest of the ingredients. Firmly pack the rice mixture into the ramekins and smooth the tops.

Place the ramekins on a tray and bake on the middle rack of the oven for about 15 minutes, or until heated through.

Let stand for 5 minutes, then carefully turn the timbales onto individual plates lined with the salad greens.

Serve immediately.

🍳 *Makes 4 servings*

65

41 Pasta Frittata

If stored correctly, leftover cooked pasta can have more uses than the famous Ginsu Knife and more reincarnations than Shirley MacLaine.

butter for greasing baking dish
1 tablespoon extra-virgin olive oil
1 clove garlic, finely minced
1 small onion, chopped
1 stalk celery, chopped
1 red or yellow pepper, seeded, stemmed,
  and diced
4 large eggs
$^1/_4$ cup milk
$^1/_4$ cup chopped fresh parsley
1 cup grated parmesan cheese
1 teaspoon baking powder
$^1/_4$ teaspoon salt
$^1/_2$ cup sliced button mushrooms or one
  4-ounce can mushroom slices, drained

Preheat the oven to 350° F. Butter an 8 × 8-inch baking dish.

In a medium skillet, heat the oil over medium-high heat and sauté the garlic until it is just browned, about 2 to 3 minutes. Add the onion to the skillet and continue cooking until it is translucent, about 4 to 5 minutes. Add the celery and peppers and continue cooking for another 4 to 5 minutes. Remove the skillet from the heat and set aside to cool.

In a large bowl, combine the eggs and milk and whisk together until well blended. Stir in the parsley and cheese. Add the onion mixture to the liquids and stir until well blended. Sift the baking powder and salt together over the mixture and stir well. Fold in the mushrooms.

Spread the mixture evenly into the prepared pan and bake on the middle rack of the oven for 25 minutes, or until golden.

Let stand for 5 minutes then serve, cut into squares.

 Serves 4

Ready to Go Pasta

Rinse any leftover undressed pasta in cold water, then shake it dry in a colander. Toss to coat with just a teaspoon of oil and store it in an airtight container. The pasta will last for up to 3 days in the refrigerator.

---

42 Remains of the Day Pasta

Throw in any veggies you have on hand. There's no need to skip this recipe just because you don't happen to have a head of endive lurking in the crisper.

> *3 tablespoons extra-virgin olive oil*
> *2 teaspoons balsamic vinegar*
> *1 clove garlic, finely minced*
> *salt and freshly ground pepper*
> *4 cups cooked pasta (preferably a short tubular pasta like rigatoni, penne, or ziti)*
> *$1/4$ cup crumbled feta cheese*
> *1 stalk celery, chopped*
> *1 red bell pepper, seeded, stemmed, and diced →*

1 small onion or shallot, finely chopped
¼ cup coarsely chopped walnuts or
   pine nuts
⅛ cup chopped pitted black olives
1 teaspoon capers
1 head endive, cut crosswise into ½-inch
   pieces

In a large bowl, whisk together the oil and vinegar until well blended.

Add the garlic, salt, and pepper and continue to mix. Add the remaining ingredients and toss to coat.

Chill the mixture for at least 1 hour, covered. This will last in the refrigerator for 3 days, if tightly covered.

☛ *Serves 4*

43 Brana's Pasta Soup

This rich, clear soup is a new and innovative twist on leftover pasta, courtesy of my friend Brana, "the reigning queen of leftover cooking."

1 teaspoon extra-virgin olive oil
1 clove garlic, finely chopped
1 yellow onion, chopped
1 teaspoon sugar
4 cups homemade Chicken or Vegetable
   Stock (see page 19)
1 cup fresh shredded spinach, well rinsed
   and any tough stems removed
½ cup thinly sliced vegetables, such as
   mushrooms (fresh or canned), zucchini,
   or summer squash

*1¹/₂ cups leftover pasta, preferably one of
   the short shapes*
splash of Tabasco sauce
salt and freshly ground pepper

In a large saucepan or small stockpot, heat the oil over medium heat. Add the garlic and cook until lightly golden, about 2 minutes.

Add the onion and sugar and cook until caramelized, or golden in color and glazed with the melted sugar. Add the stock and continue to cook until the stock is simmering.

Add the spinach, mushrooms, or whatever vegetable you might be using, and cook until the spinach has darkened in color, about 5 minutes, stirring often. Add the pasta, Tabasco sauce, salt and pepper to taste, and stir until heated through.

Serve immediately.

☛ *Makes 5 cups*

44 Beer Bread Pudding

An easy side dish for roasts, soups, or just a salad that uses flat beer and stale bread.

butter and flour for greasing baking pan
6 cups cubed stale bread
1 cup beer
4 large eggs, beaten
¹/₂ cup sour cream
¹/₂ cup milk
1 cup all-purpose flour
*one 4-ounce can chopped green chilies,
   drained*
2 scallions, chopped
¹/₄ teaspoon salt
freshly ground pepper →

Preheat the oven to 400° F. Butter and flour a 9 × 9-inch baking pan.

In a large bowl, combine the bread cubes and the beer. Toss to coat and saturate.

In another bowl, beat the eggs with the sour cream and milk until smooth. Gradually whisk in the flour, then stir in chilies, scallions, salt, and pepper. Spread the bread mixture evenly in the prepared pan. Pour the batter over the bread mixture.

Bake uncovered on the middle rack of the oven for 30 minutes, or until the top is golden-brown and a knife inserted in the middle comes out clean.

Cut into squares and serve immediately.

🍳 *Serves 4 to 6*

Bread *Winners*

Those leftover scraps or slices of bread you keep meaning to bring on your next trip to the local duck pond can easily be turned into fresh bread crumbs for your next meatloaf, pork chops, or even croûtons for Caesar salad. If stored properly, bread crumbs will last in the freezer for several weeks and will taste a lot better than the stuff in the cans, which can sometimes resemble sawdust more than an edible food product.

FOR BREAD CRUMBS

1/2 loaf stale or toasted Italian bread,
*   cut into pieces*
1/4 cup chopped fresh parsley
salt (optional)
freshly ground pepper

Place the bread cubes in a food processor and process in pulses until you achieve a very coarse consistency. Add the remaining ingredients and continue to process in pulses until it reaches the desired consistency (about 8–15 pulses).

FOR CROUTONS

1/2 loaf stale Italian or white bread,
*   thickly sliced*
1 whole clove garlic, crushed
1 tablespoon extra-virgin olive oil

1 teaspoon dried herbs, such as parsley,
*   oregano, basil, etc.*
kosher salt and freshly ground pepper

Preheat the broiler.

Arrange the sliced bread in a single layer on a baking sheet and gently rub with the garlic.

Generously brush the bread with the oil. Sprinkle the bread with the herbs, a shake of salt, and a grind of pepper.

On the middle rack of the oven, toast the bread, about 5 minutes on each side.

While the bread is still warm, slice the bread into 1-inch cubes. Although these croûtons are best when freshly made, they can be stored in an airtight container for no more than 2 days.

desserts

Fear not. Expensive ingredients or baking techniques learned only in a Parisian cooking school (*école culinaire*) do not a fine dessert make. By relying on simple formulas like store-bought ice cream enhancement or pound cake beautification, you can imaginatively provide both you and your guests with an impressive ending to any meal.

45 "Died and Gone to Heaven" Rice Pudding

Rice pudding takes about 2 hours to make, which seems like a long time when you're just trying to create an easy dessert. But before you get discouraged, just remember that the bulk of this 2-hour period is baking time and you are free to pursue other activities while your oven does the work. This recipe is engineered for comfort, not for speed.

butter for greasing casserole dish
3 large eggs, lightly beaten
1 1/2 cups milk
3 tablespoons sugar

2 cups cooked white rice
1/4 teaspoon vanilla extract
1/4 teaspoon ground cinnamon or a pinch
   of nutmeg
2 tablespoons Kahlúa or other coffee
   liqueur
pinch of salt

Preheat the oven to 300° F.

Butter a 1-quart casserole dish.

In a large bowl, mix the eggs, milk, sugar, and rice until well combined. Let stand for 5 minutes.

Stir in the remaining ingredients and pour into the prepared casserole. Bake on the middle rack of the oven for 1 hour 45 minutes, or until the center is firm.

Serve immediately.

☞ *Serves 4*

46 Banana Cream Pie

A beautiful still life composed of flawless fruit can turn into a bowl of helplessly bruised and freckled produce in just days. Don't despair: Fruits like bananas and apples are actually at their sweetest in their most abused state.

2 large eggs

2 cups heavy cream

1 cup sugar, divided

¹/₂ vanilla bean, split lengthwise, or
   ¹/₂ teaspoon vanilla extract or
   1 tablespoon Triple Sec

3 very ripe bananas, coarsely mashed

one 9-inch graham cracker crust (store-bought is fine)

dash of bourbon

¹/₂ cup toasted slivered almonds

In the top of a double boiler, or with a heat-proof bowl set in a pan of simmering water, over medium-low heat, whisk together the eggs, 1 cup of the heavy cream, and ¹/₄ cup of the sugar until blended. Add the vanilla bean or the vanilla extract or Triple Sec to the egg mixture. Cook slowly while gradually adding the remaining sugar. Stir until the mixture thickens enough to coat the back of the spoon. It might take a few minutes, but this is one of those times when patience is an active ingredient.

Remove the mixture from the heat and remove the vanilla bean. Fold in the bananas thoroughly and allow to cool for about 15 minutes at room temperature. Spoon into the pie shell and chill for at least 30 minutes.

In a large bowl, beat the remaining heavy cream with the bourbon until stiff peaks form.

Top the pie with the whipped cream and sprinkle with the toasted almonds.

Serve immediately.

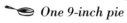 *One 9-inch pie*

VARIATION: Substitute 5 peeled, baked apples for the bananas and add $1/2$ teaspoon cinnamon to the egg mixture as it cooks.

47 Scrumptious Pound Cake Trifle

Pound cakes are the Lego building blocks of the food world. So before that leftover box of pound cake fossilizes, try toasting a few slices and constructing this simple dessert.

2 tablespoons unsalted butter

3 tablespoons sugar

$1/8$ cup Calvados, Triple Sec, Cointreau, or bourbon

1 cup heavy cream

4 thick slices leftover pound cake, toasted and cut into 1-inch chunks

1 cup hulled and quartered ripe strawberries

fresh mint leaves for garnish ➤

In a small saucepan set over low heat, melt the butter. Add the sugar and stir until the sugar has melted. Remove from the heat and stir in the liqueur. The mixture should bubble. Let the syrup stand for 5 minutes.

Meanwhile, in a small bowl, whip the cream until stiff peaks form.

Fill 4 red wine or dessert goblets halfway with the pound cake. Top the cake pieces evenly with the strawberries. Pour the sauce over the strawberries and cake, then top with the whipped cream.

Garnish with fresh mint leaves and serve.

🍳 *Makes 4 servings*

48 Coffee Ice Cream

This recipe is a beauty because it uses up cold coffee, one of the most perpetual leftovers, and it doesn't require an ice-cream maker.

> *3 large eggs*
> *1 cup heavy cream*
> *³/₄ cup sugar, divided*
> *¹/₂ vanilla bean, split lengthwise, or ¹/₂*
>   *teaspoon vanilla extract*
> *pinch of ground nutmeg*
> *1 cup strong cold coffee*

In the top of a double boiler, or with a heat-proof bowl set in a pan of simmering water, over medium-low heat, whisk together the eggs, heavy cream, and ¹/₄ cup of the sugar until blended. Add the vanilla bean or extract to the egg mixture. Cook slowly while gradually adding the remaining sugar. Stir until the mixture thickens enough to coat the back of the spoon, about 8 to 10 minutes. Remove the mixture from the heat, stir in the nutmeg and coffee, and remove the vanilla bean, if using. Cover and cool completely in the refrigerator, preferably overnight.

Transfer to a shallow pan, cover with plastic wrap, and freeze for 1½ hours.

Stir and freeze for another 30 minutes. Stir again and allow to freeze completely.

Makes 3 cups

49 Shivaun's Fruit Ice Cream

When she's not busy as an exemplary businessperson of the '90s, raising millions for the less fortunate, Shivaun Manley's mind is on matters . . . like food. This great dessert was born as a result of late-night hunger and an imaginative palate. Feel free to experiment.

> *1 pint good-quality vanilla ice cream, slightly softened*
> *1 very ripe mango, peeled, pitted, and cut into ½-inch chunks*
> *½ cup grapes, washed and halved*

Blend together all the ingredients. Refreeze, covered, for 1 hour and then serve.

 *Makes 2½ cups*

50 Glazed Fruit Sur Croûte

This dessert is as visually impressive as it is yummy. It requires little or no baking skills or extracurricular trips to the supermarket, and can be made with almost any leftover fruits.

1 tablespoon unsalted butter

3 tablespoons apricot jam or honey

$1/4$ teaspoon cinnamon

1 sheet (a bit over $1/2$ pound) frozen puff pastry, thawed

2 large bartlett pears or Granny Smith apples, cored and very thinly sliced

Vanilla ice cream to serve (optional)

Preheat the oven to 400° F. Butter and flour a cookie sheet or jelly-roll pan.

In a small saucepan, melt the butter over medium-high heat. Add the jam or honey, and the cinnamon and continue to cook until the jam has melted, stirring to blend well.

Place the pastry on the cookie sheet and arrange the sliced fruit in a single layer on top.

Liberally brush both the fruit and the edges of the pastry with all of the jam mixture.

Bake for 20 to 25 minutes, or until the pastry is puffed and golden and the fruit is lightly browned.

Serve immediately with ice cream.

Serves 4

index